AF316818

MAMA OWL, MAMA OWL, WHAT DO YOU SEE?
Written By
Alexis Renee

MAMA OWL, MAMA OWL, WHAT DO YOU SEE?

Written By: **Alexis Renee**

Illustrated By: **Nabeel Ahmed**

DEDICATION:

To both my children. This book is in reference to you. Watching you grow has been amazing, but sometimes I wish it'd slow down. To all parents, this book is for you and your child to read together and make fond memories of all the little moments.

I see baby owl staring at me.
Mama owl, mama owl, what do you see?

I see baby owl giggling at me.
Mama owl, mama owl, what do you see?

I see baby owl teething.
Mama owl, mama owl, what do you see?

I see baby owl eating.
Mama owl, mama owl, what do you see?
4

I see baby owl scooting.
Mama owl, mama owl, what do you see?
5

I see baby owl crawling.
Mama owl, mama owl, what do you see?

I see baby owl running from me.
Mama owl, mama owl, what do you see?

I see baby owl counting 1, 2, 3.
Mama owl, mama owl, what do you see?

I see baby owl brushing his teeth.
Mama owl, mama owl, what do you see?

I see baby owl off to school.
Mama owl, mama owl, what do you see?

I see baby owl smiling at me.
Mama owl, mama owl, what do you see?

I see baby owl playing.
Mama owl, mama owl, what do you see?

Mama owl, mama owl, what do you see?
I see baby owl drinking water.

Mama owl, mama owl, what do you see?
I see baby owl wearing glasses.

I see baby owl hiding.
Mama owl, mama owl, what do you see?

I see your big sister owl looking at me.
Mama owl, mama owl, what do you see?

What sound does a cat make? Does it go Meow, Woof or Moo?
The cat goes ________

What color should we paint the trunk of the tree? Pink, Yellow or Brown?
We should paint it _____
18

How many Mangoes do you see?
I see ______

What fruit is this?
A banana or an apple

It is an
____

What shape is the watermelon? Is it a circle or triangle?
Mama,this is a ________

What should we do after brushing our teeth? Should we eat a candy or should we rinse our mouth

We should ____________

What sound does
a bee make?
Does it moo or buzz?
The bee goes
____

Mama, the sky is ______
Baby, what is the color of the sky?
24

What is the
shape of an egg?
Triangle, oval, or
square?

Mama, the shape
of an egg is
____

What color is the grass?
Mama, the grass is __________

ABOUT THE AUTHOR

Alexis is from California and resides in the Midwest. She is a busy mom, working, and doing all things. In her free time, she writes as an escape. She writes poetry, songs, and her thoughts. She has written and published a poetry book and is excited to start her journey writing children's books. Stay tuned for more of her work!